BECOMING THE FULFILLED LEADER

A Story of
10 Personal Leadership Principles
Learned Through an
Unlikely Friendship

TODD STOCKER

Cannon River Press
St. Paul - Houston
www.ToddStocker.com

Cannon River Press
A DIVISION OF TODDSTOCKER.COM
P.O. BOX 25946
ST. PAUL, MN 55125

COPYRIGHT © 2015 BY TODD STOCKER

All rights reserved, including the right to reproduce this book or portions thereof in any form whatsoever. For information address ToddStocker.com, P.O. Box 25946, Woodbury, MN 55125

First edition November 2014
Manufactured in the United States of America
ISBN-13: 978-1502979827
ISBN-10: 1502979829

BECOMING THE FULFILLED LEADER

An Inspiring Story About 10 Personal Leadership Principles Learned Through An Unlikely Friendship

Todd Stocker
author of "Leading from the GUT"

Dedicated to all who seek to live a life of meaning and purpose by adding value to others around them.

"The number one regret of people on their death bed is:

'I wish I'd had the courage to live a life true to myself,
not the life others expected of me.'"

— Bronnie Ware

Contents:

Authors Note: "The Push and the Pull"	1
Chapter 1: "It's How You Respond That Matters"	3
Chapter 2: "Slow Down and Gain Perspective"	9
Chapter 3: "Pursue A 'Fulfilled' Life"	17
Chapter 4: "Stay In Touch With Those You Serve"	27
Chapter 5: "Put People First"	35
Chapter 6: "Be Aware"	43
Chapter 7: "Be Your True You"	51
Chapter 8: "Learn How to Delegate"	61
Chapter 9: "Do What It Takes To Do What You Love"	72
Chapter 10: "Always Fly High"	82
Epilogue: "Choosing A Life That Fits"	94
About the Author	98

Authors Note: "The Push and the Pull"

Contentment is a lost word in our society. Somewhere along the line, the push for bigger-better-faster has become the mantra for we who are driven to do great things. For many of us, we create a hamster wheel that provides paper-thin happiness that is tantamount to a drug-addicts need for more.

Is that really what life is to be about?

If you're looking for a leadership book how to run a company, this is not that book. If you're looking for a step-by-step process for building a team to march the new product or event forward, you won't find it here. This book is for people who want to become a person who lives a life of meaning, purpose and value.

My goal is to help balance out the 'push' with the 'pull' of life, work and everything in between. The difference in my mind is small but significant. The push is from other people and society. They mean well but may not understand who you are at your core — your true you. The pull is more internal. It is the ambition, the curiosity, the child-like adventurous spirit that plays within all of us. It beckons us forward to do great things, try great things and experience great things.

If you've ever taken a job because you didn't like the last one, you experienced the push first, not the pull. Happy are those pulled toward something greater rather than pushed away from something less.

I pray that as you are invited into this story, you are awakened to a view of a more meaningful life. As the journey unfolds, remember that you have the power to choose to become the fulfilled leader.

Chapter 1: "It's How You Respond That Matters"

The lights from the office buildings outside twinkled in dazzling brilliance against the dark night sky. To most, it would be a stunning sight. But to Mike, it was just another reminder that he was, once again, alone late at night in the only place he felt comfortable — his fiftieth floor Manhattan penthouse office.

Staring at the canvas of lights below was now a habit. It was a way to escape for him, a way to numb his mind from the pressure and stress of running a multi-billion dollar advertising firm that he built from zero to greatness. The casual outsider would envy Mike, especially the young post-university crowd who clamored for the scrap positions that occasionally would fall from the table of expansion and retirements. He knew of their admiration. Yet at that moment, all he could feel was emptiness.

Mike moved from the full-glassed window, past the leather couch to his scotch decanter warmly displayed on the curio behind his grand mahogany desk. He needed another drink. Then, he turned and looked down at the single-paged paper that was spotlighted by his desk lamp dimly lighting the darkened office.

Mike read the title of the page again, "Notice of Intent." Sinking down in his leather executive chair, he took a sip of the Balvenie and surveyed his office once again. *This might be one of the last times I'll be here* he thought. His mind numbed again.

A buyout is not what he planned when he started M.R. Worthington & Associates almost twenty-five years ago. He swirled the lone ice cube around the half-filled glass as he remembered the excitement of signing the organizing documents for the company. He recalled the quick growth that accompanied his creative design and presentation style. A smile cut across his face as the memories of adding staff and winning key accounts sparked an adrenaline rush that success often provides.

Mike looked at the few pictures neatly arranged in the far corner of his leather-topped desk. His former wife and two young boys smiled back at him from years ago. He hadn't seen them in quite some time. Why would he? After the divorce, she moved out of state and married again, a doctor this time who does medical mission work on his vacations. *How noble* Mike accused sarcastically. He missed his boys though. One now in college, the other finishing his senior year in high school, Mike was proud of who they were becoming. They reminded him of himself ... before.

He looked at the letter again.

"Dear Mr. Michael Robert Worthington,

This letter is to inform you that pursuant to our Board of Director's decision at a called meeting on May 11, The Proteus & Fen Company is taking immediate steps to purchase M.R. Worthington & Associates ... We are hopeful for a peaceful merger but are prepared to take aggressive actions according to legal and appropriate financial practices set forth in ..."

Mike couldn't read anymore. At this point, the letter was committed to memory. He thought of his executive team. Of the thousands of employees in his worldwide company, these four people meant the most to him. Each was brilliant and in high demand. But the simple thought of his team being broken up overwhelmed him. In anger, Mike palmed the paper, crinkled it up from the middle and blindly threw it toward the matching mahogany waste basket just behind his chair. The paper bounced off of the adjoining cabinet and onto the floor, missing the basket by three feet.

"Do you want me to get that for you, Mr. Worthington?"

The voice from the half opened door startled Mike and it took a few moments to regain his composure.

"Oh, I'm sorry," the voice said. "I didn't mean to interrupt you. I'll come back later."

Mike looked toward the partially opened but now closing door.

"Wait." Mike said. "I'm just finishing up. You can come in."

The door opened slowly and a slender man stepped in.

"This late at night, I didn't think anyone was still here." The man said.

Mike looked back down and half-smiled. "No one is." Mike said, self-deprecation intended. The man raised an eyebrow, stepped in, picked up the crinkled "hostile take-over" letter, put it in the basket and dumped the remaining assortment of papers and empty envelops into a larger container on a cart just outside the door. 'Craft Cleaning Services' was imprinted on its side.

Mike found himself watching the man's work. Even emptying his trash, Mike noticed that this man didn't just randomly dump the papers, he landed them in the places of the bin that would create optimal efficiency. The man was even whistling as he did so.

"I'm sorry," Mike said. "I've been a bit on edge lately."

The man paused. "I understand. There's always an element of stress in every moment of life. It's how you respond that matters. Have a good night." Before Mike

It's How You Respond That Matters

could process the statement and respond, the man put the wooden trash bin back in its place, flashed Mike a smile and quietly slipped out into the hall, closing Mike's door behind him. Mike could hear the man's whistling diminish and finally disappear down the opposite hallway adjoining his assistant's workspace.

There's always an element of stress in every moment of life. The words bounced around Mike's mind for a few moments. *It's how you respond that matters.* He knew the man's words were true, especially now. Especially for what he knew he had to do on Friday. He was not looking forward to it.

Chapter 2: "Slow Down and Gain Perspective"

The automatic drapes opened predictably at 6am, letting the morning sunlight cut a path through the spacious luxury condominium. "Time to wake up, Michael," Lola said. Mike ignored the prompt and turned away from the sunlight. "Michael, its time to wake up," Lola said again a few minutes later.

"Lola, off!" Mike snapped at the digital system named 'Lola' that controlled everything from his alarm to his shower temperature. The system was a gift from one of his clients. Mike's firm helped increased their sales by 36%, putting the tech company on the market map. An all expenses paid vacation to Belize and 'Lola' were part of the expression of appreciation to Mike.

Mike rolled over again. He remembered that he was alone. Even though it had been years since he unintentionally shipwrecked his marriage and family, a dull ache still lingered. He pushed out the thoughts, flipped off the freshly pressed Egyptian linen sheets and sat up.

"Lola, half-caf coffee."

"My pleasure," the artificial assistant replied. Mike sat at the edge of his bed listening to Lola start the Keuring coffee machine in the all-stainless steel kitchen. He listened to the outside traffic 25 stories below and subtly wished he didn't have to go to the office.

The phone call interrupted his thoughts. Mike waited for Lola.

"Michael, Steve Bryer from Jackson and Hunt Law Firm is calling. Should I answer it for you?"

"No Lola." Mike said, not wanting to start the day talking with the lawyer whom he held on retainer.

"Okay, Michael. I will tell him you are unavailable."

Mike stepped down off his bed platform, across the dark marble living room floor and up two steps into the kitchen area. The coffee was hot, just how he liked it. He took the cup into the adjoining exercise room and slipped into his workout gear. The morning routine was one of the only normals in his life. For him, it provided the necessary mind-clearing that he needed to start the day.

An hour later, he was in his Lamborghini Aventador, weaving through moderate traffic toward his company's building. On normal days, he would be listening to the morning business reports. The last few days, he preferred classical music.

After leaving the high performance vehicle with the valet, Mike was greeted outside the building by Todd Harper, his Vice President of Marketing and one of Todd's assistants. Mike always joked about how odd it was that a marketing company needs a VP with the same title. Todd always kidded back about quitting. Now it wasn't that funny.

Mike listened to Todd as they walked.

"Mike. So, I just heard from Mary in Minneapolis and she is preparing our statements to the press and our employees. She seems to think that 'less is more' but I think we need to be direct and defiant. We gotta beat this thing."

"Let's see what Mary comes up with and we can tweak it from there." Mike said. "The most important thing right now is confidentiality. Everyone senses there's something going on but they don't know how serious this could be. We can't say anything until the time is right and that time is coming soon."

Todd looked back at his assistant whom he trusted without question. Then they entered through the rotating doors. Immediately the group was met with a flurry of "Good Morning Mr. Worthington. Good morning Mr. Harper." Mike and Todd responded robotically, "Good Morning" until they were safely inside

Plan For The Future But Take It Step By Step

the executive elevator with the doors closed behind them.

The momentary quiet was broken as Todd said, "Mike, I know you're concerned about the employees and you've told us that people matter, but if you push to have the re-hire protection clause in the paperwork, you just might jeopardize our personal positions with outside corporations." Mike bit the inside of his cheek. "I don't know about you, but I've worked too hard to give up my career because of some lower-level staffer. Besides, their pay-scale is deemed re-hirable by the market. They can find other jobs."

Mike was appalled at Todd's insensitivity, especially with his assistant standing right behind him. But he also understood. He knew the mortgage payment on Todd's multi-million dollar mansion would rival the national budget of many foreign cities. Mike's condo was no small chunk of change either. The emotional numbness had returned.

"Todd, we'll take this step by step. Remember, we all worked out a plan with Steve and the transition team and we'll follow it until the horizon changes." The digital bell announced the floor and the doors opened. "I'll see you at the meeting this afternoon," Mike said as he stepped off the elevator and through the glassed doors etched with his name.

"Good morning, Mr. Worthington. How goes the battle?" Gayle was in her late thirties and held her age well. Her beautiful blonde hair and deep chocolate eyes made potential clients feel welcomed and loved all at the same time. Gayle was Mike's Executive Assistant and probably his most trusted employee and friend.

"Good Morning Gayle," Mike said. "Fine, thanks. Just another day in paradise," he said sarcastically.

"Great. Steve Bryer called and needs you to call him right away. You have two more certified letters on your desk from Proteus and I need you to sign the requisition paperwork for Carl's meeting with the Board."

"Yes ma'am," Mike said saluting as he pushed through his office door, leaving it cracked open. He took off his suit jacket and plopped it on the overstuffed leather chair in the sitting area of his office. Glancing out at his world-class office view, he returned to his desk and began pressing through the emails, phone calls and letters, each seeming to move his company closer toward oblivion.

The afternoon executive meeting went as expected. The main agenda item was the impending battle for the future of the company. Todd kept banging the drum for self-preservation. Beverly Westinger, VP of Operations concurred while Carl Wynn, VP of Business and Finance said that the executive buyout option and stock transfers that Proteus were offering were well above normal market standards. Paul Easting, VP of Customer Service, sat quietly at the end of the couch and simply took notes which he was prone to do. Like Paul, Mike also withheld his opinions and instead played devils advocate by lofting leading questions to his team.

Finally, Todd said, "You guys, it's a losing battle! Proteus is too powerful for us to fight! I don't know about you but I'm going to get my affairs in order!" With that, Todd crumpled up the previously distributed meeting agenda and left Mike's office. An awkward pause later and with Mike's permission, the rest of the team gathered their things and exited the office leaving Mike to stare out the window at the pigeons who had taken up residence on the corner of the window ledge outside.

It's how you respond that matters, Mike thought slowly.

He could here the stately janitor's voice in his head. An unexpected calm came over him. In similar meetings, Mike would blow up at his team, threaten pink slips or unload extra assignments which were usually useless. This time, he took a moment to gain perspective and repeated the words under his breath, "It's how I respond that matters." Mike then added, "How *am* I going to respond?"

Chapter 3: "Pursue A 'Fulfilled' Life"

He watched the sunset from behind his desk. The orange and red hues illuminated the floor, walls and ceiling and made the ice in his scotch sparkle like the diamond he bought for his wife when life seemed simple.

"Another late night," the familiar voice said as a statement rather than a question. Mike's attention jolted toward his half-opened door.

"Looks like it," Mike responded.

"Mind if I come in and take care of your office for you?"

Mike looked around the space. Even though he prided himself in his orderliness, he did notice various trade magazines and a thoroughly read Wall Street Journal in disarray on the coffee table centering the sitting area.

"Sure. Come on in." Mike said.

"Thank you." The janitor opened the door, bypassed an opened envelop that had fallen from Mike's desk and began straightening up the sitting area of which Mike had just examined. The janitor was whistling as he worked.

"By the way," Mike said. "Thanks for the advice last night."

The man stopped whistling but kept cleaning. "Advice? Refresh my memory."

"Well, you said that what is really important is how you respond to stress and not the stress itself."

The janitor turned to Mike and scratched his forehead and smiled. "I said that. Wow, that was pretty brilliant if I do say so myself." Then he chuckled.

"Well, it sure helped me from losing my cool this afternoon." Mike stood up from his desk and extended his hand toward the man. "I'm Mike. Mike Worthington."

"Yes, I know," the janitor said as he wiped his hand on a cloth from his pocket, looked Mike straight in the eye and shook his hand. "Nice to meet you officially, Mr. Mike. My name is Charles but most people just call me Chuck."

Mike noticed that Chuck moved like a professional and had a firm but not too strong grip. "Please to met you as well." Mike said. Chuck went back to his work.

"How long have you been working here?" Mike said as he leaned against his desk and cupped his scotch. Not that he cared but shallow conversation was better than digging through financial statements at this point.

"Oh, for a while now. It's a good job and helps pay the bills." Chuck said. "I imagine you know what I mean."

"Yes sir. I do." Mike said. The thought raced through his mind that paying bills might be difficult in the days to come. As he watched Chuck work, he noticed that there was excellence in the way he did it. He didn't just dust around the ten thousand dollar glass centerpiece that was shaped like two intertwined smooth edged flames. He lifted it up enough to run his dust rag underneath it. "Say Chuck, can I ask you something?"

"Shoot."

Mike hesitated but then continued. "Well, I don't want to offend you and you can tell me to stop if I'm prying, but why are you a janitor?" As soon as the words left his mouth, his ears told him he shouldn't have said anything. So he tried to compensate.

"What I mean is you seem like an intelligent man and I've already seen you do things with excellence."

"Well, that's a fascinating question." Chuck said in a manner which communicated non-offense. "But let me ask you a question, if you don't mind." Mike raised his glass in approval. "Why did you choose to be a CEO?"

Mike was a bit stunned at the question. Climbing the corporate ladder was everyone's dream, wasn't it?

Money. Power. Fame. Options. Bonuses. Women. Parties. Mike could make a long list but chose not to verbalize it at the risk of more potential offense.

"I don't know if I chose it. It just sort of happened. I'm a driven kind of guy. I like the excitement, the risk and the benefits if you know what I mean."

Chuck smiled and nodded his head in acknowledgement as he began dusting the glassed coffee table.

"Besides," Mike continued, "look at this office. Who wouldn't want this?"

Chuck chuckled to himself which Mike heard.

"What's so funny?" Mike said.

"Oh, I don't know." Chuck said. "Seems like you should be pretty happy."

Mike was waiting for the next question which never came. So Mike answered it anyway. "Well, it's a bit difficult right now. We have a lot going on in the company and I've got to figure out a way to keep us afloat."

"You have a family?" Chuck said.

"Of course. I mean, the wife left a few years ago with my boys and moved to North Carolina but we still see each other, occasionally." Mike felt a sweep of guilt, knowing that the split was mostly his fault. "What about you?"

"Been married for forty-two years. Four kids, eight grandkids and our first 'great-grandy' on the way." Chuck said.

Mike was impressed. After his divorce, he always thought that marriages didn't last in this day and age. He took another swig of scotch.

"Well, I guess success and families don't mix." Mike said.

Chuck's brow furrowed. "How do you mean?"

"It seems if you want to be successful and raise a family, you have to sacrifice on both ends." Mike felt pretty confident in his statement.

Chuck tucked his dust rag in his back pocket. "So you think you're successful?"

Now Mike was offended. "Of course I am. I mean, mostly."

"Mr. Mike, I don't want to barge in but I think you are a bit clouded in your thinking." Chuck didn't wait for Mike to respond. "You see, if life has taught me anything it has taught me not to pursue 'success'."

Now Mike was confused and sensed a challenge.

"Really." Mike said as a statement and not a question. Chuck wasn't phased.

"I'm serious. People who pursue success often end up being failures. People who want to define their life as 'successful' will mess up what makes life beautiful. Success is a horrible adjective for life. A person can only be successful at *part* of something not *all* of something."

'Success' Is A Horrible
Adjective For Life

Pursue Fulfillment

Now Mike was really confused and his furlough brow exposed it. Chuck noticed.

"Let me try and explain it in a different way," Chuck said. "'Success' can only be defined as the accomplishment of a single goal or purpose." Chuck pulled a dust rag from the back of his painter's pants walked to the deep-wood bookshelf to the right of the window. "Now, if my goal is to dust this bookshelf and I only dust this one shelf, would I have successfully achieved my goal?"

"Obviously not," Mike responded.

"What if I dusted the whole thing, would I be considered a successful janitor?" Chuck asked.

Mike was beginning to think that this was a trick question but he answered it anyway. "No, well, yes. I mean, you finished that part of your job but the rest of the office is messy."

Chuck smiled and said, "If someone could be successful in reaching a position in a company but a complete failure in his personal life. Would that person's life be a success?"

Mike knew the inference was personal. "What are you saying, Chuck? Are you saying that with everything that I've achieved, with everything I've accomplished, my life is a failure?"

Chuck smiled, looked at the floor and then back up at Mike.

"If you don't mind me saying so, it seems to me you have a lot to learn for being a 'success'." Chuck continued respectfully. "Mr. Mike, the kind of life you want is not a successful life but a *fulfilled* life. One with meaning and purpose and one that matches how you've been designed and one that adds value to others around you.

Now Mike was evaluating his own life. Achievements and failures flooded his thoughts and battled for prominence.

Chuck continued, "Life is more than occasional successes. In fact, most people don't realize that they hold the power to make the kind of decisions that lead to the kind of life they want. That's why I asked you why you *chose* to be a CEO. Whether you knew it or not, you made small decisions along the way to get you where you are today — the good and the bad."

Mike took another sip then said, "So what you're saying is that the mess I'm in now is a result of the choices I've made in the past."

"That's mainly how life works. There are times when what happens to you is the result of others and there are also times when God directly allows or causes events to happen. But mostly, where we are today is because of how we respond to our life experiences and the choices we make."

Mike remained quiet. Chuck's comments both irritated and interested Mike.

Chuck paused and looked intently into Mike's eyes. "Seems to me you're at a crossroads of sorts, Mr. Mike." Chuck picked up the envelope he'd passed earlier. "And if there's anything I can do to help, let me know." With that, Chuck stepped out of the office and closed the door behind him.

Mike found himself staring out the window again. The memories of starting M.R. Worthington and Associates were exciting. He and two others venturing out in a small rented office in an office park outside the city. Winning their first account and making major decisions over cups of cheap coffee. Good times. Now Mike didn't do any creative work. His days were filled with meetings and talking with the top 7% of the company's clients.

Chuck was right he thought. *I am at crossroads in all areas of my life and tomorrow's meeting isn't going to make it any easier.*

Chapter 4: "Stay In Touch With Those You Serve"

The meeting was at 7am. Early for most, but for Mike, he was already a few hours into his day.

Todd, Beverly, Carl and Paul walked into the executive board room together, all holding their morning coffee mugs in varying forms. They took seats on one side of the Mahogany conference table. Mike was already sitting at the head and the scones and danish that Gayle's picked up fresh were already displayed in the middle to soften the meeting. Steve, the attorney, came in a few minutes later. The Proteus transition team was yet to arrive.

"Well, this should be fun," Todd blurted out. Mike ignored him.

"Mike, how do you think this will go down?" Paul asked.

Mike leaned forward in his leather chair, rested his elbows on the table and folded his hands in a stately manner.

"Here is what I know. Proteus wants to suggest the first rounds of lay-offs to help make the transition 'smoother' — their word, not mine." Mike turned to Beverly under which Human Resources fell. "Bev, you're going to have to walk hand in hand with the HR directors on this since they'll be issuing the changes." Beverly agreed.

Steve passed out neatly bounded packets to the team. "What I'm handing out are more of the details of Proteus's requirements and our position in the negotiations." Mike didn't open his. "The purpose of this meeting is as Mike said. The release or repositioning of staff, employees and the executive team."

At that moment Gayle opened the door and escorted three equally dressed men into the room. Skinny suits accompanied their disheveled hair juxtaposed against Mikes team of professional suits and hundred dollar hair cuts. They were much younger than Mike or anyone on his team and exuded the kind of confidence that only comes from positions of power. Mike and his team stood respectfully and exchanged introductions, pleasantries and the normal chit-chat that is meant to break the ice and set a casual tone. During this time,

Steve and the lawyer from Proteus swapped cards and set printed agendas in front of each table position.

Josh was the lead of the Proteus team and never broke eye contact with Mike. Once seated, Mike scanned the table and spoke first.

"Well, everyone let's begin. In front of you is ..."

"I think we can just cut to it, don't you think, Mike?" Josh interrupted. Mike was stunned at Josh's callus rudeness and found himself with his mouth open. Without waiting for an answer, Josh continued.

"We all know that Worthington has been successful for many years under Mike's leadership and that many companies and individuals have benefitted from the firm's work. If you look at the financials on page sixteen of the packet that Steve handed you, you'll see that earnings have flattened over the last nine quarters which indicates a shift in how you're doing business or in the market's dullness to your old ideas and lack of innovation."

Carl frantically flipped to the page referenced. He knew that costs had been up and the market fluctuations had taken its toll but 'flattened' wasn't a word he'd use to describe the condition. Mike sensed the immediate tension in his team especially Todd who was about to go across the table on this youngster.

"Josh, first of all, thank you for the kind compliment. Our company takes pride in the excellence of its work and the servicing of its customers." Mike said.

Know Whom You Serve

Josh didn't hesitate. "The problem is this, Mike, and no offense to your hard work. You don't know your customers anymore." Mike sensed Todd shooting at glance at him. Josh continued. "For example, your Bennington Sports package designs are at least 3 years old and simply a copy of your work with Zero Soda Company. You clutter, the market simplifies. We think that the way you do business and the product you give your clients has run its course. Yet there is so much potential and opportunity at the core of who you are. Our company thinks we can step in, take what's good about Worthington and transform it into the company it was born to be."

Todd stood up with his fists clench and knuckles down on the table. "So what you're saying is that you want to disassemble our company, take what you want and kill everything else!" Mike leaned over and put his hand gently on Todd's forearm. Startled, Josh leaned back in his chair and the partner to his left leaned forward and folded his hands in front of him.

The partner waited until Todd sat down and said, "Todd, its time for a change and you know it." Being an arrogant man, Todd took offense that the Proteus team spoke so casually to them, using only their first names. The partner continued, "Mike may be a great guy and your company feeds you well. But it's dying and the whole market smells it. We just want to help."

Mike felt sick. Not by the comments he took personally but by the false sincerity of the Proteus partner. *He sucks at acting* Mike thought.

"We're prepared a public statement of transition that we're ready to submit to the shareholders of Worthington," The Proteus lawyer said. "It is on page 5 of your packet." Mike's team flipped the page open. "It highlights the past experience, the present condition and calls for a future change of the leadership team by a simple majority vote." Mike looked at Steve, waiting for him to jump in. Steve diverted his eyes.

"So what you're saying is that this is transition by proxy, is that it?" Mike asked.

"Yes," the lawyer said. The Proteus team kept silent.

"And you're confident that the shareholders feel the same way?" Mike said and then looked at Steve who was fidgeting with his four-hundred dollar fountain pen.

"We've done some offline interviews and found a growing discontent in your leadership." Josh said. Mike kept looking at Steve who did not return the glance.

"Steve," Mike said, "tell me you didn't know about this."

Steve remained uncomfortably silent.

At that moment, Mike knew he'd been undermined. He knew that he'd been betrayed and he wasn't sure who on his team was trustworthy.

Over the next few hours, Josh and the Proteus team made 'recommendations' for a 'healthy' transition and outlined the potential severance packages that would accompany employees who resigned over and against those who didn't.

After the basic schedule of transition was understood, Josh and the Proteus team gathered their portfolios and left the room.

By this point, Mike wasn't standing three inches away from the conference room window looking aimlessly at the beckoning skyline. No one said anything for a few moments. Then, one by one, Mike's team left quietly. Lastly was Steve. Before he exited, he met Mike at the window and began to say, "Mike, I know how this looks."

Mike abruptly put up his hand.

"There's nothing to say, Steve," Mike said.

With that, Steve left and Mike continued to stare, lost in his thoughts and wounded to his core. He churned over the past few hours in his head. The thought of people losing their jobs because of his incompetence made him sick. Then he began to think about what Josh said at the beginning of the conversation.

Have I really lost touch with my customers? Am I really that disconnected with the market? Mike needed to breathe. He needed space. He needed a change of scenery and he knew just the place to be.

Chapter 5: "Put People First"

On this day, the sun's warmth felt nice. Coney Island was always the place that Mike breathed the best. Smog aside, the memories of family vacations triggered as he saw the water, the sand and the boardwalk littered with kids — five school busses worth. His wife and he once rented a small apartment a few blocks off the beach and spent countless hours with the kids playing in the water, riding the rides and eating hot dogs from *Nathan's Famous* until they couldn't eat anymore. It was a golden time.

Mike strolled along the walk, boards creaking under each step. The constantly scavenging birds soared above him, wondering if Mike's pockets held stale pieces of bread on which they could feast. Like a child, Mike pretended to throw a piece in the air. They darted and dashed at the 'nothing' that came their way. Mike smiled.

"Mr. Mike." Chuck's firm and cheerful voice broke his play. "What brings you to this part of the island?"

Mike suddenly felt like he'd met a long lost friends. "Chuck! Crazy that we'd meet here." Mike extended his hand and shook Chuck's. "After this morning, I just need to clear my head. You?"

"I always bring the grandkids here on Fridays. They are over there by the water." Chuck leaned into Mike and pointed to a group of four children, two playing in the water, one digging in the sand and the littlest holding a foam noodle that was twice her size. "Those kids are who keep this old guy alive." Mike noticed the huge grin on Chuck's face.

"Sounds like a good way to spend a Friday." Mike said.

"Sure is." The two continued to stroll slowly along the boardwalk. After a brief pause, Chuck said, "Sounds like this morning wasn't so great? If you don't mind me asking, what's going on?"

Mike glanced at Chuck then back down at the now concrete path on which they strode. He wondered if he should let Chuck in on more of what is happening at the firm. Chuck seemed like a man of integrity and now, like a confidant, so he decided to open up.

"Well, the basics of what's going on is public knowledge so I guess it's okay to tell you." Mike felt better verbalizing the disclaimer. "Our team met with another company to talk about the possibility of joining our forces to dominate the market in advertising."

"Ah yes. The Proteus & Fen Company." Chuck said. Mike was surprised.

"Yes. So you've heard."

"I try to keep up with the companies I serve." Chuck said. Mike again was impressed.

"Well, the gist of our meeting this morning was about the transition in regard to employees. Which departments are we keeping? Which ones are being restructured and which ones are being dissolved?" Mike looked over at Chuck and read in his face that he was weighing the options.

"And then there is the Executive Team," Chuck said, again to Mike's surprise.

"Yes," Mike said. "Most of the other employees we can accommodate in other departments and the ones that would be let go have the experience and skill to connect with other companies. But my team and their direct teams are a different story."

Chuck kept looking down at the concrete path and said, "Management always gets the first axe."

"Precisely," Mike said. "Frankly, there are a few on my direct team that I shouldn't have hired in the first place."

"Why is that?" Chuck said. Mike paused, sensing that he was about to violate team integrity but somehow he knew he could use someone with whom to share — in confidence of course.

"In the beginning, we were all focused on building a great company, But now, I just think that some are only in this thing for themselves."

Chuck nodded slightly and groaned in understanding. Mike continued.

"I mean, they're good people and they've achieved a huge level of success — some by hard work, others by favors and family status. That's not necessarily bad, but it seems to me that our team has lost its direction. We have forgotten our core focus and why we exist."

"And what was that core focus?" Chuck asked.

Mike suddenly stopped walking. Looking up at the waves slowly lapping into shore, he realized that even he didn't remember why his own company existed.

"I don't know," Mike said, stunning himself.

The two walked on for a few more moments without saying anything.

"Mr. Mike. Do you remember the other night when I was just about to clean your office?" Mike didn't remember any specifics but nodded anyway. "There was an opened envelop on the floor by your desk and it was obviously the first thing I could've picked up when I started. But what did I do instead?" Mike remembered.

"You went right to the coffee table that looked like a tornado had run its course!"

"Exactly," Chuck affirmed. "Now, here's the thing. While the envelope was first for me, it wasn't first for you. What I mean is, I notice what seems to bother people and I try to attack that first. For you, it was the coffee table that didn't look that messy to me. But to you, Mr. Mike, it was a disaster and it really bothered you." Mike grinned and nodded because Chuck had pointed out one of Mike's pet peeves — a messy coffee table.

"See, you know what I'm talking about," Chuck continued. "In my years, I've learned that trying to serve people in the way *they* need and want always results in a positive outcome — eventually. My momma always told us kids, 'Put people first and you'll be first among people.' That's good advice right there," Chuck said smiling and poking his big finger into the middle of Mike's chest in a friendly, man-to-man way.

"Put people first and you'll be first among people," Mike repeated under his breath. "I think that's want we've been missing! I mean, what *I've* been missing."

"There you go," Chuck said.

"Not only in my work, but personally as well." Mike felt tears push up into his eyes. "I guess I've been so caught up in my own 'success' that I've forgotten how to love and serve others."

"It's easy to do," Chuck affirmed. "I've done it in my own life as well — too many times to count."

Mike suddenly felt the urge to dig more.

Put People First And You'll Be First Among People

"What *have* you done in your life Chuck?" Chuck's brow furrowed. Mike continued, "I mean, here you are, a janitor in a building and you just happen to know a lot — and I mean *a lot* — about big business, the cut-throat corporate world and personal development. Right from our first encounter, you've been giving words of advice to me that don't come from reading a book or watching Youtube videos. It's like you've lived all this before — in my position. I don't even know your last name." Mike noticed Chuck grinning as if he was holding back a story that seemed to crazy to be true.

Chuck folded his arms, glanced over at his grandy's and cocked his head to one side. "Mr. Mike, there is a lot about me that I don't like to share. Yes, I was in the business world for quite a while. Even had a little success. But there are things I've done and left undone that have hurt many people — me being one of them. So let's just say I've come to a point in my life where I'm choosing to serve rather than be served."

Just then, little arms grabbed around Chuck knees from behind. "Gotcha!" It was one of Chuck's grandy's.

"Gotcha back!" Chuck reached down and pulled the youngster up onto his shoulders. "Mr. Mike, this is Logan. Logan, this is Mr. Mike, a good friend of mine."

This little one smiled at Mike and said nothing.

"It's great to meet you, Logan," Mike said, smiling back. Logan shyly diverted his eyes and tucked his head behind Chuck's.

"Well, Chuck, I've got to get going but thanks for the conversation," Mike said.

"Absolutely and you're welcome. You've got a lot on your shoulders right now my friend and I appreciate the opportunity to help in anyway I can — that may even include cleaning your office." Chuck said smiling, extending his large hand to shake Mikes. Mike obliged and headed back to his car

As he pulled from the parking lot, Mike noticed that his spirit seemed lighter and more directed. Chuck's grinning face flashed into his mind and he was grateful for this random janitor who just happened to be brilliant.

Chapter 6: "Be Aware"

It was rare for Mike not to work on Saturday's and this one was no different. The day usually found him reading a market analysis report or a cash-flow summary and then spending hours online setting up meetings for the next week. This day, Mike decided to do something he hadn't in years. He decided to go shopping — not online, not through his assistant but personally, walking the streets, going store to store and actually purchasing items.

Just be aware Mike told himself as he opened the door to the medium-sized, very popular store called The Toy Shoppe located on upper 10th. He was looking forward to being in a toy store again since it was this industry that helped catapult his company at each level of their growth.

A shop bell clanged as the lighting and colors splashed his senses. On the right of the store a yellow and green framed display held what looked like furry oversized tennis balls. Behind those were floor to ceiling wooden shelving containing baskets full of age-appropriate playthings. On the left were stuffed animals and dolls — all were sporting an embroidered, printed or painted smile. "It feels like an olden-days shoppe" Mike said under his breath.

"Hi! Welcome to The Toy Shoppe." Mike was greeted by a cute, young brunette wearing an apron. "My name's Amanda. Have you stopped by before?"

"Uh, no." Mike was caught off guard.

"Well, feel free to look around and if there's anything I can help you find, please let me know," Amanda said, handing Mike a 3x5 sized colorful card with simple printing at the top that read, "Here's Your Map To The Toy Shoppe." Mike found it easy enough for a 5-year old to understand.

Mike made his way to the balsa wood model plane section. As a kid, his father and he would spend nearly every summer Saturday, building these footlong replicas. He found a Curtis P-36 Hawk Fighter, pulled it off the neatly stacked shelf and headed toward the check out area. Two other shoppers were in line ahead of him, one grandmotherly woman and a young mom holding the hand of her toddler who was bouncing up and down in response to being overstimulated.

Be aware Mike reminded himself again. The cheerful gal behind the counter engaged the grandmother and the young mom in chit-chat. What caught Mike's attention was the cashier came around from the counter, bent down on one knee and said to the toddler, "Well hi there. I love your shoes!" to which the child giggled and bounced even more.

Mike's turn. He put the model plane box on the counter.

"Hi. Did you find everything you wanted?" the gal said making precise eye contact with him.

"Yes, I did, thanks," Mike said.

"Great." The gal picked up the box scanned the barcode and said, "Oh a P-36! Great choice. You're going to love the final outcome." Mike noticed that she was actually sincere. Her love for the toy — all the toys — was genuine.

"Say, I noticed you said, 'I love your shoes' to that little kid ahead of me" Mike said to the gal who was putting the plane into a brightly colored bag "I got this at The Toy Shoppe."

"Thanks for noticing," the gal said. "The reason is we want to add value to everyone who comes in. I know that shoes are one of the first things that toddlers have control of as they are growing. So I wanted to make sure that little girl knew that I valued her choice."

"Brilliant." Mike said.

"Just simple," the gal replied, smiling and handing him the bag. "I'll see you next time."

"Thanks," Mike said.

"You're worth it," the gal said, causing Mike to stutter step as he pushed through the large frosted glassed doors out onto the street. *You're worth it* Mike repeated in his mind. *That's awesome.*

Mike began heading to another toy store up two blocks and over three from this one. As he walked, he began to wonder how his company compared to this one. He knew the difference between his and theirs was in the 'product,' but he also wondered if M.R. Worthington valued their clients. Did his people generally love the company and believe in what they could accomplish? Was there an atmosphere of innovation and excellence? Did he know his customers wants, needs and desires? Mike felt a bit nauseous because his own answers seemed to leave him empty. *Maybe the Proteus guys were right* he thought.

Toys Now was a staple in the city. It was started by Italian immigrants at the turn of the century in a response to the heavy influx of children arriving from other lands. Expanding to more than 600 locations nationwide, their marketing was some of the best. As a grad-student, Mike applied to the company but was rejected through a form letter.

The automatic sliding doors whipped open as Mike stepped onto the rubber sensor matt. At grocery-store

Always Notice The Little Things

They Are The Key To Adding Value To Others

size, Toys Now held every toy a kid could ever want. The bright florescent lighting illuminated the unending rows of displays. The environment reminded him of Home Depot. Mike found himself humming to the music that was piped over the speakers attached to the ceiling. The tune lyric of *Wake me up before you go, girl* hung in his mind. Quite odd for a toy store.

Be aware Mike thought again.

Mike strolled through the store, noticing everything from the color schemes of the displays to how the customers responded to the cluttered shelves and misplaced items. Mike began looking for the aisle that held the model airplanes like the one he purchased at The Toy Shoppe. Suddenly, he awkwardly realized that he was carrying the other store's bag through the aisles of its competitor.

"Hey," said a young man re-stocking a shelf behind Mike. "Can I help you find something?"

"Well, I'm looking for the model airplane section."

"Cool. You're close. It's just 3 aisles down, past the dolls on the left hand side. Row 23," he said. Mike noticed the man eyeing his bag from "The Toy Shoppe." He also noticed that his eyes squinted slightly which sent a negative message to Mike.

Mike walked down the main aisle trying to follow the young man's directions. Yet, he still couldn't find the planes.

"Excuse me," Mike said to an over middle aged woman trying to organize the Barbie section. "I'm looking for the model planes. Can you show me where they might be?"

"Yup." The woman started walking toward another aisle, not saying a word to Mike. "There they are" she said flippantly pointing to half an aisle filled with them.

Mike saw the P-36 at a cheaper price than The Toy Shoppe but with orange mark-down stickers plastered on the face of the box. He picked it up and walked to the front of the store where 3 checkout lanes were staffed. Waiting in line behind people with grocery carts filled with discounted toys, Mike finally reached the counter.

"Wow, you're busy," he said to the clerk who didn't look up and simply scanned Mike's purchase.

"It's always like this on Saturday's. I'd rather be at the beach," the girl said chewing her gum. After she was done, she glanced up at Mike and asked, "Anything else?"

Mike shook his head without saying a word. They completed the transaction and he left the store.

The contrast was startling. Mike's awareness revealed many things but mainly that environments make a difference — not just the physical space but the relational environment as well. As he sat in his car, Mike looked at the two bags that he plopped in the front seat. For him, he'd definitely go back to the one.

Chapter 7: "Be Your True You"

Once again, Monday's meetings ran late as Proteus correspondence seemed to hit the office every hour. Even in the chaos, Mike couldn't shake his conversation with Chuck on Friday and his experiences at the toy stores on Saturday. In one weekend, Mike felt his attitude and energy for moving forward rising. He even found himself looking forward to talking with Chuck, if the chance presented itself in the evening. But for now, Mike had to deal with the personnel challenges at hand.

Steve Bryer, the attorney that was supposedly helping Mike's company, now only communicated through email or his secretary. Not even Gayle, Mike's assistant, could get him to answer the phone. Instinctively, Mike knew that Steve was setting the table for his jump to a Proteus position.

Todd, Carl and Paul were also becoming more difficult to pull together for meetings. Mike sensed they were working a 'looking out for number one' strategy as well. Only Beverly, Mike's VP of Operations, seemed to be focused on her work.

At 7:30 pm, Mike walked down the executive hallway toward his office at the end. All lights were off except Beverly's.

"Hey Bev," Mike said as he gently tapped on her office door that was slightly open.

"Hi Mike," Bev said looking up from the laptop that was poised on a docking station. "I'm revising some of the language in the Proteus operations transition proposal they sent over this afternoon. So far, it looks okay but we need to make sure …"

"Bev," Mike interrupted. "Your family needs you at home, more than I need you here." Bev was always diligent about her work, sometimes at the expense of her family. Normally, Mike would say the obligatory 'great job' and let her continue but tonight, he felt differently about it.

"I know," Bev responded. "I have a few more pages to cover."

"Bev, it can wait till tomorrow. As your boss, I'm kicking you out," Mike said with a gentle smile, raking his fist and thumb over his shoulder. Bev smiled as well, agreed, gathered her things and left the office.

"Have a good night, chief," Bev said.

"You too."

Mike watched her walk down the hall and open the large double glassed door just as Chuck was pushing his cart through it.

Mike was delighted and walked down the hall to greet him.

"Chuck! Perfect timing! I need to tell you what I did after our conversation Friday."

"Rob a bank?" Chuck quipped.

"Funny. No, I went shopping."

"Wow!" Chuck said sarcastically, "Sounds like fun."

"It actually was. I went to two toy stores to see what I could learn about the customer experience." For the next few minutes, Mike relayed everything he could about the two stores and what he noticed. Chuck listened as they walked to Mike's office.

Finishing, Mike said, "I even built the model plane to put on my shelf in the office. It's in my car." Mike felt proud of his accomplishment when Chuck broke his silence.

"So let me ask you," Chuck said. "If you were an employee of The Toy Shoppe and you walked into Toy's Now, how do you think you'd feel?"

Mike looked up in thought and then said, "I'm not sure I can answer that. On one hand, I'd feel good because my store was more personable and more inviting. But on the other hand, my store wasn't as popular or successful as Toy's Now and we didn't have as large a selection." Mike felt good about his answer.

"Okay, switch it around. A Toy's Now employee walks into The Toy Shoppe." Chuck said.

"Same thing. There are pros and cons to both scenarios — things in which each do well and each could do better. It depends on their purpose and demographic."

"Correct you are. But that wasn't the point of my question." Mike was confused. "Did you notice that you compared the two experiences to each other and drew conclusions based on that comparison."

"Of course I did. That's what you asked me to do," Mike said.

"Not exactly but your answer illustrates something that we all do. Compare."

Mike was still confused. "What's wrong with comparing?"

"Do you remember one of our first conversations? I walked in when you were at the start of this Proteus deal and I told you ..."

"... It's how you respond that matters," Mike said, proud that he remembered.

"Exactly. But what I didn't tell you is that your response should be based on your true you."

"My true me?" Mike questioned.

"Yup. Let me explain. The problem for most people is that they are stuck trying to achieve happiness by comparing their lives with other people. Bad plan. This is the reason they buy things and do things that they can't afford. They are trying to impress other people rather than finding and sticking to what makes them come alive. I've known many people who were promoted right out of what they loved to do, because everyone else said they should do it. They were pursuing ..."

"Success," Mike finished.

"Whoa! Good memory," Chuck said eyeing Mike up and down.

"And success is a bad adjective for life," Mike said.

"Correct again!" Chuck said.

Now, Mike could relate. He was perfectly happy years ago when he and his wife had their second child and he was working as the lead director of a creative arts department of another marketing firm. Mike was an artist at heart. He came alive when he was staring at a blank artist page, realizing what he drew could become anything he imagined — especially when it came to toys. His talent betrayed him to the lure of success. He was told by his friends and extended family that he should start his own marketing company and his now ex-business partner wouldn't quit pointing to others who had done the same and were a hugely 'successful.'

Chuck interrupted Mike's stroll through his mental photo album. "I was listening to a speaker one time and

Comparing Kills Clarity

he summed it up nicely. He said 'there is no win in comparison.[1]' If I compare my life to others and find it better, then I'm arrogant. If I compare my life to others and find it lacking, then I'm desperate. I've repeated that phrase over and over in my head."

"But you can't just ignore competition in the business world. It provides a gauge — a marker — as to what you're doing and where you should be going, right?" Mike said hesitantly.

"It can. Wasn't it helpful for you to compare the two toy stores?" Chuck said.

"Absolutely."

"But what was especially helpful was that they are not in the same industry as you. So the comparisons from which you were drawing were not on a tactical level but more on an experiential level. You walked away with some learnings that you could take back to your company. Learnings like 'valuing people is important,' 'stay true to yourself' ..."

"... And don't carry a competitors bag into another store," Mike joked.

"Exactly" Chuck said laughing. "But I think you see what I mean. In business and in your own personal life, comparing yourself to someone else can be helpful from a benchmarking standpoint, but you can't let it re-shape who you were created to be. You always have to go back

---

[1] Andy Stanley, Northpoint Resources, http://bit.ly/1ygo3ON

to your own original purpose — your true you. That is defined by what makes you come alive! Then the way you play out that purpose can adapt given the environments in which you find yourself."

Mike was getting the picture but wanted to bring it back into the business world "Can you give me an example from business?"

"There are thousands but let me give you one from a subject that I love — food!" Chuck rubbed his belly and Mike chuckled. "Many people don't remember that at one time, Chipotle Mexican Grille was mostly owned by McDonalds, financially speaking anyway."

Mike vaguely recalled reading about that business arrangement in the Wall Street Journal ten years ago.

"McDonalds was watching this little unique restaurant chain grow at a steady rate. The leadership team thought it'd be good to get into the burrito business in order to enhance their brand and product offerings and they wanted to compete in the ever growing Mexican Food chain arena. At that time, McDonalds had also acquired interests in Boston Market and Donato's Pizza — two food chain areas that were also growing. But after being in the burrito business for a while, the leadership divested all of its interests in other restaurants so that they could focus on their core purpose — being and advancing the McDonalds chain."

"That sounds a bit like my company," Mike confessed. "We have lost sight of our core purpose — our true us

— because we've been comparing ourselves to others in the industry. I remember when we set out as a small company that we were going to be the foremost marketing and advertising experts for toy stores. But seeing what others were doing, we began going after clients in so many different markets that we never were great at any one thing. We're spread so thin and have lost touch with who we are — or were."

"It happens in business. It happens in life," Chuck said.

Mike felt a bit like a student in a university business class. "Is there going to be a test on this?" Mike again joked.

Chuck got serious.

"Yes and most likely, it will be soon." The change in Chuck's demeanor and the tensioned pause that followed left Mike motionless.

"Have a nice night, Mr. Mike." Chuck pulled out his rag, wiped the top of Mike's framed MBA diploma by the door and stepped out.

What did he mean by that? Mike was soon to find out.

Chapter 8: "Learn How to Delegate"

Days passed but for Mike, it felt like years. Every hour presented yet another mandate or change from Proteus to Worthington. Financial projections, employee accounting and department restructuring plans flooding onto Mike's desk with little help from Steve, his all but defunct attorney.

Yet Mike noticed that while the conversations and transition decisions were becoming more intense, he was feeling less stressed, more focused and able to make wise decisions that put people first, sometimes at the expense of the bottom line. The last handful of nights, he was even out of the building before Chuck came to clean.

"Mike." Gayle's voice hummed through the intercom sitting on his desk.

"Yes, Gayle."

"Josh from Proteus wants to set up a lunch meeting today at 12:30, just the two of you."

Mike's brow furrowed. He knew that legally, it would be best to have a third party attend.

"Did he mention 'why'?"

"No, just that it was only for you and him."

Mike paused. Josh's request was extremely out of the ordinary for these types of transitions. *Be my true me. My true me can negotiate better in person rather via email.*

"That's fine Gayle. Put it on my calendar and let me know where we're meeting" Mike said, leaning into his gut more than his lawyer.

"Will do." Gayle's voice was professionally friendly no matter what the circumstance.

Mike checked his watch. With a few hours before the meeting with Josh, Mike decided to prepare. He picked up the latest Executive Assessment Timeline that the Proteus lawyers create and send every three days. This one came this morning.

As he was scanning it, there was an entry that simply said, "Point Leader Transition Invitation." The date was today. Mike felt a small knot growing in his gut. He knew that that entry was directly related to the lunch meeting with Josh. He was soon to find out.

Novatny's was an Italian eatery that catered to the high-end financial crowd. Even Mike only went there on special occasions — not because of the price, which was spendy, but because it was unique.

The valet was more than happy to park Mike's Lamborghini and Mike paid him well for the extra care.

"Good day, Sir," the long-tuxedo suited doorman said. Mike nodded and stepped in. The brightly lit room was three quarters full with expensively styled executives from all parts of the city. Scanning the silken draped tables for four, Mike saw Josh and Josh stood in welcome.

"Hi Mike, thanks for coming." Josh extended his hand and smiled warmly. Mike accepted hesitantly and the two sat down.

"Thanks for the invitation, Josh but I have to say that given our situation, isn't this a bit odd?" Mike said motioning between the two of them.

Josh smiled and said, "Yes, I know this isn't the standard protocol for what our two companies are doing, but I felt that an open conversation would be good." Josh interwove his fingers and set them on the table. Mike sat back in his chair.

"You know," Josh continued, "you and I are a lot alike."

"How so?" Mike said.

"Well, both of us are passionate about what we do. Both of us have a vested interest in making this transition work and I know this might surprise you, but both of us care about the people we serve." Mike *was* surprised but kept listening.

"Now, we've had only a few face-to-face meetings and everybody else has been working to get this deal done. I just thought the two of us should have a chat about ultimate outcomes without the flurry of emails, reports and Skype conversations. I want to hear what you want in this deal."

Mike sensed that Josh was setting him up with an empty concern about Mike's goals.

"Let me ask *you* something, Josh," Mike said. "Why is Proteus investing so much in taking down my company?" The question hit the table like an anvil. "I mean, you could swallow up a dozen or so other companies much small than us and more than accomplish your financial and market percentage goals. Why Worthington?"

Josh sat back in his chair and took a sip of water without unlocking his gaze at Mike.

"Mike, let me tell you a story," Josh said. "When I was in grade school, my dad owned Hamline's Groceries in the Bronx." Mike recognized the name. Josh continued. "It was designed for a simple, customer-focused experience and had a unique flair for making folks feel at home. I spent hours before and after school helping out, getting to know the people and learning the basics of the business. Watching my dad do what he loved, even though he barely made ends meet, meant the world to me. He saved up enough to put me through college and grad school and then I came back to Hamline's to work with my dad. My intent was to eventually take over the store so that he could slow down into retirement and I could develop Hamline's into a national brand."

"Sounds like a good plan," Mike said, "but what does this have to do ..."

"My dad and I worked hard those first eight years together in the business. We got to a point where we decided to expand and open up more stores. In order to do so, we needed help — specifically in the marketing and advertising areas. So guess who we hired?"

Mike suddenly remembered. He remembered the first time he walked into Hamline's and how it felt like a hometown grocery store — a jewel in the midst of a deteriorating neighborhood. He remembered having the initial meeting with Josh and his dad in the makeshift conference room above the floor of the store. He remembered Josh having a huge vision for where this 'mom+pop' store could go and he also remembered what happened.

"I remember, Josh. I remember how much I liked Hamline's and what you guys were doing and wanted to do."

"Yes, but do you also remember how your company sucked every last penny from my dad and assigned one of your new-hires to lead a marketing and advertising

The Decisions You Make Today Affect The Outcomes Of Tomorrow effort that not only killed our first expansion store but also caused such stress on my dad that he had a heart-attack? Do you remember that?" Josh's voice raised a bit.

Mike did remember. It was at a time when Worthington was securing larger accounts and Mike didn't want to focus on such a small piece of business like Hamline's. As a result, he assigned the Hamline's account to an intern not a new hire. Mike did not want to make that correction out loud. "Josh, I'm sorry about your dad and there were some mistakes that we made."

"Mistakes? I'd call them broken promises that were bordering on being illegal!" Josh took control of his demeanor. "My dad poured everything into Hamline's and you left him penniless. Did you know that he had to sell Hamline's a year later to a guy who turned part of it into a tattoo shop?"

Mike didn't know that and now he felt bad about it. After an uncomfortable silence, Josh said, "After it all went down, I reconnected with a friend I met in school about a job. He is the son of the founder of Proteus. Long story short, they put me on their Executive Fast Track and here I am — making a bid for the company that ruined my dad's life."

Mike was stunned at Josh's admission.

"So this whole thing is personal, is that it?"

Josh half-grinned. "I like you, Mike. I really do. It's not personal, its professional. I don't have a grudge against you because I understand business. I understand a leader's responsibility to allocate resources in the best way they think at the time. I also understand that delegation has to happen. So, no. It's not personal, but I believe the best recourse that also happens to be good business for us at Proteus is to take over Worthington, 'taking the best and leaving the rest' — as my dad would say."

No wonder Josh wanted this conversation off the record Mike thought and now he knew where this was heading.

"So here's what I want to happen," Josh continued. "I want you to resign by next Wednesday from Worthington, effective at the first of the month." Josh's unemotional words stunned Mike. "In doing so, you'll get a nice severance and I've already lined up some key positions for your executive team which some have already accepted. I think you know who they are." Mike knew.

"And if I refuse?" Mike said.

"Then this deal will officially go hostile and we'll disband Worthington in a way that leaves thousands of your people unemployed. You get zero severance and Worthington will go down in history as another failed company because the leader — that'd be you — refused to adapt to changing conditions." Josh said.

Mike felt the bottom of his eyes sharpen. The primal parts of his mind wanted to reach across the table and rip this kid to shreds but his higher intelligence refused that urge.

"Well, there it is," Mike said. "'Your cards on the table' sort of speak." Josh sat back and folded his arms.

"Oh," Josh continued, "and I'll need to know by this Friday morning. I have a meeting with my team at 10."

Mike pursed his lips, stood up and walked toward the door.

"Don't forget," Josh said again, "by Friday."

Mike stepped out, handed his ticket to the valet and mindlessly watched the traffic dart by him only a few feet away. He was still stunned by the lunch meeting. He rehearsed the past mistake with Hamline's and how he had completely turned that account over to the intern without any direction or guidance. *Part of a leader's job is to delegate not abdicate.* Mike thought of Chuck because that would be something he'd say.

Mike's thoughts were interrupted when the vibration of his cell phone gently shook his blazer's breast pocket. The facial icon showed Gayle.

"Hi Gayle," Mike answered.

"Hi Mike. Sorry to interrupt you but I received a call from the admitting station at New York Methodist Hospital. They said they have a patient there who asked for you. It sounded urgent."

"Who was it?" Mike asked.

"The patient told them to tell you it was Chuck the Janitor. Do you know who that is?"

Mike felt the adrenaline flood through his body. "Thanks Gayle. I'm on my way."

Chapter 9: "Do What It Takes To Do What You Love"

Mike arrived at the hospital within minutes. He pushed through the turn-style glassed doors and rushed over to the closest desk behind which sat a receptionist. As he approached, he realized he didn't even know Chuck's last name.

"Without a last name, I can't direct you to the right area, sir," the receptionist said.

Turning around, he saw a family hurrying in through the same doors. Mike recognized the little boy that he'd met a few week prior at Coney Island. It was Logan. He walked over to Logan's mother whose face was creased with a worried look.

"Hi, my name is Mike and I got a call from this hospital saying Chuck was here. Do you know where he is?"

The mother looked surprised but then realized that this was the 'Mike' that Chuck mentioned weeks prior.

"Oh, Mike. My name's Stacia. He's just coming out of emergency surgery. They're moving him from recovery to room 2405."

Mike and the family headed into the elevators. No one said a word. Mike looked down and noticed Logan staring up at him, studying his face. He smiled back, trying to reassure the boy.

After what seemed like eons, the elevator bell rang, the doors opened and he group scurried to the 2400 wing of the floor.

"There it is," Mike said, picking up his pace and leaving the family behind. Nurse attendants were moving in and out of Chuck's room, each time making sure the door mostly closed behind them. Mike caught one and asked, "Can we go in?"

"Not yet. You can go and wait in the waiting room. We're just getting Mr. Craft stabilized and he should be ready for visitors soon."

'Craft,' that name sounds familiar Mike thought. The family joined Mike and he led them to the end of the hall. Several people were clustered around the room. Some were quiet, some were talking softly and others were gazing blindly at a TV mounted in one of the corners. Mike found a few chairs and pulled them together.

Once settled, the group didn't say much except for some basic introductions. Mike found out that Logan's family was from Chuck's oldest son. In the brief conversation, Mike realized he asked Chuck very little about his family — he didn't ask Chuck much of anything on a personal level. Mike felt bad about that.

After several minutes, the nurse indicated that it was okay to see Chuck but that Chuck wanted to see his family first. Mike graciously understood and deferred, choosing to get a cup of coffee from the machine at the far end of the room. As the coffee was slopping into the styrofoam cup, the mention of 'W.R. Worthington' caught his attention. On the TV, a news report was alerting the world that Mike's company was in merger discussions with Proteus and Fen, potentially creating one of the largest marketing and advertising firms in the States. The report was neutral as all news should be but the public awareness made Mike feel helpless. *What am I going to do* Mike thought.

"Dad wants to see you," Stacia said, interrupting Mike's internal conversation.

Mike nodded, headed down the hall and into Chuck's room. The ledge by the window held several bouquets of flowers and a planted vine with balloons that read "Get Well" on them. Chuck was in an ambulatory bed, half propped, with his head resting on the sterile white pillow. Tubes and wires connected his arms to several monitors, one of which beeped with obnoxious consistency.

Chuck open his eyes to a squint as Mike approached his bed.

"Hey, Mr. Mike," Chuck said in a scratchy voice.

"Hi Chuck. How you feeling?" Mike said because that's what he thought he should say.

"Well I'm not ready to run a Marathon but I'm getting along," Chuck said and then coughed. Mike helped reposition his pillow. "Seems my past line of work is catching up to me."

"What do you mean?" Mike said.

"Well, the Doc says that the cancer is getting pretty bad. He says that its probably from all the chemicals I was around in my younger days."

"Oh, Chuck. I didn't know," Mike said with sincere concern. "Can they do anything about it?" Mike asked.

"Too late for that. Besides, I've lived a full life and one of my joys has been to get to know you." Chuck coughed again and struggled for air.

"Let me get the nurse," Mike said.

"No, all they do is poke me like a Thanksgiving turkey. I haven't seen you for a while so they can wait. I want to hear what's been happening at work," Chuck said.

Mike hesitated, not wanting to add more stress to Chuck. But he also knew that Chuck found joy in hearing and analyzing the events surrounding the buyout. So Mike shared a condensed version of the past weeks which culminated in the conversation from which he'd just come.

"So as you can see," Mike said, "I have a pretty hefty decision to make. Should I fight this thing or should I step aside for the betterment of the other employees?"

"And maybe for yourself?" Chuck added. "You already know the answer, Mr. Mike."

"Yes, I guess I do."

Chuck pushed himself up on the bed.

"Mr. Mike, I've taught you a lot of things in a short amount of time. They are lessons I learned growing up and especially when I owned my own company." Just then a nurse came in to replace the almost-empty clear bag that was hanging of a metal post to Chuck's left.

"How you doing, Mr. Craft?" the nurse said as she worked. Suddenly, Mike realized who this brilliant janitor was.

"Craft? The Craft Company! The cleaning company you work for! You are Charles M. Craft?" Mike said.

"The very one," Chuck said.

"You were one of the most successful entrepreneurs of your time. In school, I read a case study on the beginnings of your company and how you provided cleaning services and products for hospitals."

"Yes, we did. It was an amazing journey."

"But why are you ..."

"... just a janitor?" Chuck said. Mike sheepishly smiled.

"Well, you must not have followed the full story. Our company was the fastest and healthiest company in our industry. We expanded from cleaning services to chemical innovation and development." Chuck coughed again and then continued.

"Just like many other companies, we let the success overshadow our attention to detail and safety. We simply got sloppy." Chuck stopped to catch his breath while Mike waiting.

"Then, as everything froze after 911, we had to cut costs and decided to move part of our production down to the Dominican Republic. It worked great at first. We employed hundreds of folks at the plant in between San Pedro and Santa Domingo. But then, people in a small city that we employed down there became violently ill. Seems we had been dumping a by-product chemical into a river that fed the main water supply downstream. Kids were dying. People where losing their sight. It was bad. When I found out about it, it shook me to the core." Chuck stopped again.

"Why are you telling me this, Chuck?"

"I tell you that to say this. The day I found out what my company was doing and the thousands of lives I hurt simply because of my laziness, that day ripped me apart. Working with the board, I immediately shut down most of our business and stuck with the one piece that was

Do What You Love
But Do What It Takes To
Do What You Love

core to my heart — the cleaning services branch. I also resigned as CEO, sold off my shares and laid low for a good number of years. Only recently decided to start cleaning for my own company."

"No offense, Chuck, but why?" Mike said.

"Because I love people and I love serving them. Sometimes you got to love what you do but do what it takes to love what you do." Mike repeated the phrase in his head. *Do what you love, but do what it takes to do what you love.*

"For me," Chuck continued, "I realized that by creating businesses, I was able to serve people in unique ways. But when I found out that the very business I created to make people's lives better actually made them worse, I had to do what it took to get back to doing what I love. It's the 'doing what it takes' that is the hard part."

Mike understood and nodded in agreement. In light of the decision he was about to make, 'doing what it takes to get to doing what he loved' was going to shock his world.

"Chuck, if there is anything I can do, please let me know, okay?" Mike said as Chuck's family trickled back into the room.

"Is that an order, Mr. Mike?" Chuck grinned.

"You bet it is, my friend," Mike said as he reached out and shook Chuck's hand. "See you soon." Then, he turned and started walking out of the hospital room.

"You're going to be okay, Mr. Mike," Chuck said in a wheezy voice. "You're going to be okay."

Mike smiled and headed toward the elevator. His mind swam in the deep wisdom of Chuck which also seemed to provide life-direction given the earlier conversation with Josh. Mike smiled again because it was now clear what needed to be done and why he felt so at peace.

Chapter 10: "Always Fly High"

The phone call came in the late afternoon on a cold, rainy Tuesday. Uncustomary for Gayle, she walked into Mike's office unannounced. Mike was at his desk highlighting portions of the latest Proteus injunction that outlined how the stock acquisition and transitions would occur.

"Mike, sorry to interrupt but there's a call on line three that you need to take."

"Okay, thanks." Mike sensed the urgency in Gayle's voice and immediately picked up the phone and hit the green flashing button on his desk phone. Before he could say anything, he could hear a voice shaking on the other end.

"Hello, this is Mike."

"Mr. Mike? This is Stacia, Chuck Craft's daughter. We met at the Hospital last week."

"Yes, Stacia. I remember," Mike said, already knowing what she was going to say.

"My dad ..." Stacia's voice cut out. Mike paused. "My dad passed away this morning."

Even though Mike knew it was coming, to hear the words felt like a sucker punch to his gut. He paused for a moment to collect his thoughts and then spilled out a few words.

"Oh, Stacia. I'm so sorry. Were you all there with him?" Mike said.

"Just mom and me and Logan," Stacia said. Mike sat back in his over stuffed leather executive chair picturing that chubby-cheeked little boy darting glances from behind his Grandpa's head at the beach where they first met. Stacia continued. "He just fell asleep with no coughing and the hospice nurse said he didn't feel any pain. Before he died, he made me promise that I'd let you know."

Mike felt overwhelmed as tears pushed up through his eyes, rolled down his cheeks and splatted on the now, non-important Proteus papers on his desk.

"Thank you Stacia. Would you email me the arrangements for the funeral. I'd really like to come," Mike said. With that, Mike and Stacia exchanged information and he hung up the phone.

Mike looked at the quickly drying tears spots that were now staining the noisy papers in front of him. Motionless, he heard nothing but the laughter of his janitor-friend echoing in the empty place of his mind. Looking up, Mike was drawn to the rich skyline outside his office windows. Mesmerized by the raindrops that spotted on the glass, he quietly thanked God for the opportunity to have met such a man.

"It's not supposed to be this way," the business-suited pastor with perfect hair said as he motioned to the white-pall draped casket that held Chuck's body. The pastor's words reverberated through the large auditorium that normally seated 2000 souls but today, swelled to 3000 that video overflowed into the atrium.

"God's original plan was not for death, but for life. It is this kind of life that Jesus gave to Chuck and He offers to the whole world." The pastor's words reminded him of the sermons he heard as a kid when he attended church with his grandparents. *Those were easier times* Mike thought as he sat close to the back next to the sound both that hosted four volunteers, each intent on removing distractions and enhancing Chuck's celebration of life service.

As the pastor's message unfolded, Mike's eye's walked up and down the aisles of the massive space. He wondered about each family's story and how they were connected with Chuck. Some looked like business colleagues from the past, others resembled family while others were most likely members of Chuck's church. To Mike, it didn't matter. He was surprised and amazed

Your Life Impacts More People Than You Realize

that any man's life could have such an impact on so many people.

As the last hymn — "Amazing Grace" — was played triumphantly by the worship team, Mike felt overwhelmed. At first he didn't know why. Maybe it was emotion, or sadness, or his own exhaustion. Then Mike realized what Chuck had been trying to tell him throughout the past few months. A key measure of a person is not in what he does, but who he is and how his life adds value to others.

That is why so many people are here Mike thought, *because Chuck added more value to others than what he wanted for himself.* Mike looked down at the handout that he'd folded in half part way through the service. He looked at the picture of Chuck on the front, surrounded not by money, or houses or plaques that proclaimed his business prowess, but his 'grandy's' — the little kids into whom Chuck poured his heart — his life.

The service ended and Mike solemnly followed his row out into the aisle and down the hall to the Atrium that was set to host every person in attendance, and then some. The hundreds of white-clothed tables were neatly set and catering rows filled with food outlined the comfortable room. The line of people was already growing at a steady rate.

Mike surveyed the space, recognizing many of the same families from the worship center. Not knowing anyone and feeling a bit out of place, he decided not to

Add More Value To Others Than What You Want For Yourself

stay. He turned toward the double doors that led out of the atrium when he felt a tug on his pant leg. Looking down, he saw the bubbly grinning face of Logan, Chuck's grandson. Stacia was standing a few feet away.

"Hey little man," Mike said, stooping down on one knee to connect with him eye to eye.

"Hi Mike," Stacia said, moving straight in for a hug. Mike stood and obliged without any reservation.

"Oh, Stacia," Mike said holding her gently by the shoulders. "How you doing?"

"We're okay," Stacia said. "We've known for years that this day would come and so we were prepared ... as best as we could be, I guess."

"Planned or unplanned, Chuck's passing still hurts," Mike said.

"Incredibly. Mike, he was a wonderful dad and he talked so highly of you."

Mike's gut hurt again and he felt the tears pushing. "I enjoyed getting to know him over the past months and I've learned so much from him, Stacia."

"I'm glad I caught you because he gave me this to give to you." Out of the purse that hung loosely over her forearm, Stacia lifted a small dark-leather moleskin journal and gave it to Mike. It looked like it was fresh out of the wrapper. Mike flipped through the pages to find most of them empty save a few that showed evidence of use.

"Thank you, Stacia. I'll treasure it for sure."

Stacia put her hand on her Mike's forearm and locked eyes with him. "Mike. Chuck's last words were for you. He said, 'Tell Mr. Mike to fly high.' Do you know what that means?"

Mike thought of his recent toy shopping experience, the P36 model plane he purchased and the conversation he had with Chuck about the traps of comparison.

"I think I do, Stacia. Thanks for that."

Mike and Stacia hugged again. Then Mike patted Logan's head, said, "Take care," and walked toward the exit. As he did, Mike opened the journal to the few pages that held ink. It was Chuck's handwriting. On the first page, Chuck's voice lifted from the page as Mike read.

Dear Mr. Mike,

I don't know if you're reading this because I've taught you all I know or I'm dead — which sounds pretty morbid, even to write. But inside these pages, I'm endeavoring to journal our conversations and the thoughts that I've given to your current situation. Each page has the lesson we talked about at the top plus a brief overview of our conversation. Hopefully, this will be helpful to you as you look back and evaluate your life. Most likely, there are empty pages at the back. Those are for you to complete as you continue your journey.

Life is a wonderful gift, Mike. Never forget that. It is filled with adventures and mysteries. It is constantly teaching you lessons on fulfillment and it won't stop because you've experienced a set back. Life even tells you that setbacks are necessary to take leaps forward.

It has been my pleasure to know you and I pray that God would use the following pages to help you live the life you were meant to live.

Peace!
Chuck

Mike looked up from the journal as tears staining his cheeks once again. The words echoed Chuck's heart and sank into Mike's. Quickly, Mike flipped to the next page, eager to see what else Chuck wrote.

At the top of the page was written 'It's How You Respond That Matters.' Mike remember that key lesson. Beneath the title was a detailing of their first, late-night meeting. Chuck noted his first impressions of Mike and that the signs of over-drinking showed on his face. Mike touched his cheek, realizing that he hadn't had or wanted a scotch for a few weeks.

The next page of the journal was titled "Slow Down and Gain Perspective." The entry described how Chuck found Todd's crumpled paper agenda from the executive meeting and how Chuck noted that to him, it seemed like Proteus was not giving Worthington enough time to transition.

Each page was like that one. Each held indispensable truths, teaching and observations from

Chuck about Mike's life that could serve as a business class outline.

Mike flipped to the last page on which Chuck wrote at the top, "Always Fly High By Adding Value To Others." The page was empty. It dawned on Mike that that was Chuck's next lesson to him. Yet, Chuck never had the opportunity to share it.

Even with the empty page, Mike had an idea where Chuck would've gone with the lesson. The metaphor for 'Always Fly High' would've been taken from the Curtis P-36 Hawk Fighter that Mike bought weeks before on the Saturday at the toy stores. Mike knew that Chuck was a man of integrity and that living your life in that way would be to 'fly high.'

Mike also knew 'Adding Value To Others' was simply what Chuck did every moment of every day. To Chuck, serving people was the greatest act of love — of adding value to people's lives. Thinking about how he could make someone's life just a little better was a key priority for Chuck.

Mike had an idea that would honor Chuck and accomplish the last lesson. He stuffed the journal into his coat pocket and headed for his sports car. Unlocking the small trunk that barely held a brief case, Mike pulled out the completed P-36 Fighter and headed back to the reception.

As he entered the large hall, he headed toward the main tables elegantly set in the front. There he saw

Chuck's family, Stacia and Logan. Mike's stealth movements brought him to Logan's chair. With the family unaware of Mike's presence, Mike bent down, winning Logan's attention.

"Logan, I know that you loved your Grandpa very much," Mike said tenderly. "And I know that he love you to. So I want to give you something from me but also from him."

From behind his back, Mike revealed the perfectly built plane model. Logan's eyes double in size and a smile cut across his face.

"Logan, when I was your age, I loved model planes — especially this one. So I want to give you this plane as a gift from me." Logan looked up from the plane and locked eyes with Mike.

"And Logan, there's something I think your Grandpa would want you to know," Mike said, putting his hand over the pocket hold the journal.

"Logan, I believe your Grandpa wants you to Always Fly High. No matter what happens, always be good, always do the wise thing, always help others, Always Fly High."

Logan nodded slightly and Mike wasn't sure if he understood. No matter. Mike delivered the message that he believed Chuck would've wanted.

Mike stood, looked at Stacia who was smiling back at him from her chair, and left the room.

In those moments, clarity cut through the noise of the past months — years. With Proteus demanding a decision about his resignation, Mike knew exactly what he wanted to be about. He knew that he held the power to choose the kind of life he wanted to live and he knew that meant making a tough decision.   His next step would change the trajectory of his current life-path, and while terrifying, it was a good thing.

Epilogue: "Choosing A Life That Fits"

Mike stood staring at the crisp one-dollar bill neatly framed and hanging on the rough bricked wall over the light switch of the renovated fire-house that was now his office downstairs and his home up-lofted. The proceeds from the sale of his luxury condo years before more than covered its purchase and renovation. *Liquidating is fun,* Mike had to remind himself over the past years since his resignation from Worthington and the subsequent dismantling of that company that cost him everything. Now he stood in an open floor planned building older than a century which the college-aged crowd called 'hip'. Its high ceiling and large room was often used on the weekends by local Asheville, North Carolina artisans since the adjustable lighting and grungy atmosphere created an environment perfect for their live-music, coffee-house venue.

After his resignation, Mike transitioned quickly to a simpler, less corporate lifestyle and was even thankful that the buyout went the way it did. Proteus was harsh but still had a heart. Mike was allowed to start his own company after 6 months without a non-compete contract but was given a gag-ruling on the former M.R. Worthington operations. His new company focused on that which Mike was passionate — Toys. Stabilized on three pillars of Toy design, marketing and advertising, the ToyCraft Design Company was focused, simple and added value to companies wanting to create toys with integrity. Mike was back to his roots.

"Hard to believe it's been four years already Gayle," Mike said as he pulled out a hanky from the back pocket of his jeans and dusted the bill's plaque that read, 'First of Many - The ToyCraft Design Company'.

"Sure is," Gayle said as she brought her coffee to her wood door-topped desk. Mike was glad that Gayle and her family were willing to make the move. Being in real estate, her husband quickly built a new clientele and Gayle benefitted as they were now closer to her parents who settled in Ft. Meyers, Florida.

Bev also made the move with Mike. Unlike Gayle's, Bev's husband simply quit his job and is a stay-at-home dad who found his love in writing children's books.

The life change held more added benefits for Mike than he could've planned. Being close to his former wife and sons provided a reconnection to her as a friend and a restart of his relationship with the boys. Mike even felt comfortable enough to hire his eldest son, Cody as part of his team.

Mike walked to his simple desk positioned squarely on the hand-made rug he bought from the crafter in the building next door and leaned against its thick wooden edge. He watched Gayle on one side of the room handle incoming calls and scribble on her note pad as she had at Worthington. On the other side, Cody and Bev were standing at the large white board that engrossed half of the brick wall. Back and forth, they bickered about color schemes for the presentation they were to pitch to the company named 'Habbery' who specialized in stuffed animal toys for Children's Hospitals. Mike's contentment forced a smile.

Mike looked down at the well worn leather journal that Chuck left him. Mostly filled, the pages now were a guidebook for Mike. Over these years of starting ToyCraft and redirecting his life, he'd added and referred to the words of wisdom many times.

Mike picked up the treasure and felt the smoothened texture of the book. He held it tight as he once again observed his new life unfolding slowly before him. The years bore witness to poor decisions based on even worse motivations. Yet, Mike knew it was what needed to be.   In that moment, he was thankful to God that a seemingly random meeting between a janitor and an executive would turn out to be the greatest encounter in the world.

About the Author

Todd Stocker is an author, speaker, personal and professional life coach. He has led organizations ranging in size from half a dozen to several thousand people and has provided training for companies and organizations such as Hilton Resorts, US Airlines, American Express and Concordia University.

Todd has and trained thousands in the areas of personal development, leadership and team building. He is the author of 5 books including "Leading From The Gut," "Refined," and "Rosemont" which is being scripted as an on-screen movie. He currently leads the team at Trinity in Hudson Wisconsin, a ministry organization with two thriving campuses, a large education program and community service initiatives that impact local and international people groups. He is the founder of ToddStocker.com which helps ordinary people discover, develop and deploy their purpose in life.

Most importantly, he is a devoted family man who loves to spend time with his wife and children and they live in Woodbury Minnesota.

For more information, go to
www.ToddStocker.com.

IF YOU LIKED THIS BOOK, CHECK OUT THESE BY TODD
[YOU CAN PURCHASE THEM ON AMAZON.COM]

"Rosemont." Forty years ago, ROSEMONT was a thriving town until a mysterious murder. It is all turned around by a 11 year old girl who encounters tragedy, forgiveness and restoration. And it all begins in a town called ROSEMONT.

"BreakThrough Weight Loss: 5 Proven Ways To Get And Stay Healthy Today" All of us would like to be in better shape and feel healthier. Todd lost 45 pounds using the methods he outlines in this book.

"Leading from the GUT: 3 Practice of Healthy Leaders" Leadership doesn't begin with what you do but with who you are. This eBook describes 3 practices that every leader should work on to become and healthy and long-lasting leader.

"Refined – Turning Pain into Purpose." We all experience loss at some point in our lives. Whether simple or complex, the emotions can leave us wondering if there is any purpose in it at all. As a refiner, Todd realized that the process of refining gold and silver mirrors the process of grief that ultimately reveals it's purpose in our lives.

"Dancing With God – First Year Thoughts on the Loss of My Daughter." All of us go through loss. This incredibly emotional book chronicles the year following an accident that killed Todd's oldest daughter. Join him on his journey of loss as he was comforted by the Lord in amazing and powerful ways.

"Manners Matter – 10 Table Manners Every Child Should Know." Eating a meal together as a family can be a wonderful opportunity for building closer relationships and having fun at the same time! Our book, "Manners Matter" can help begin conversation with your youngster about proper table manners and why they are important.

"Infinite Playlists – How to have Conversations, not Conflict, with your Child about Music." This is a handy guide to healthy conversation between parents and kids. Writing as both father and music-lover, Todd calls parents to recognize music as a gift from God so they can help their kids determine the emotional, physical, and spiritual influences of their song choices. He offers a balanced look at the difference between Christian and secular music, and gives practical guidelines parents and kids can follow to choose appropriate music-together.

www.ingramcontent.com/pod-product-compliance
Lightning Source LLC
Chambersburg PA
CBHW051811170526
45167CB00005B/1975